塞·格瑞瑟艺术作品集

石头
木头
文字

Stone, Wood and Words,
Collection of Sy · Gresser's
Art Works

中国文联出版社

感谢以下朋友，由于他们的协助，本书才得以问世，但愿书里的这些形象能够回报他们付出的努力和关心。

高若意　张　敏　沈凌华　陈复声　邹昆凌　姚建华　丁立平　张建荣　刘　路
Del Lewis　Edward Paris　Sarah Shay　Jesse Cohen　Bill Moore

Special thanks are due to those friends who helped to produce this presentation of one artist's statement, The images in the book hopefully rewarded their efforts and care.

Gao Ruoyi, Zhang Min, Shen Linghua, Chen Fusheng, Zou Kunling, Yao Jianhua, Ding Liping, Zhang Jianrong , Lui Lu Del Lewis, Edward Paris, Sarah Shay, Jesse Cohen, Bill Moore.

主　　编：高若意（美国） 　　　　　陈复声	Chief Editor: Ruoyi Gail Gao（U.S.） Chen Fusheng
中文翻译：高若意 　　　　　张　敏（美国）	Translators: Ruoyi Gail Gao Zhang Min（U.S.）
编　　辑：邹昆凌 　　　　　姚建华 　　　　　丁立平	Editors : Zou Kunling Yao Jianhua Din Liping
装帧设计：张建荣 　　　　　杨翠华	Designers: Zhang Jianrong Yang Cuihua
赞　　助：沈凌华	Sponsor : Shen Linghua

Title: Stone, Wood and Words
Author: Sy Gresser
Publisher: Zhongguo Wen Lian Chu Ban She.
Distributor: Quan Guo Xin Hua Shu Dian.
Executive Editor: Wang Dongsheng
Press: Yunnan Xin Wen Tu Pian She Yin Shua Chang
Copies: 500
ISBN7-5059-4365-0/I · 3400
Price: RMB80.00

图书在版编目(CIP)数据

石头·木头·文字/塞·格瑞瑟 著.–北京：中国文联出版社，2006.8

ISBN 7-5059-4365-0

Ⅰ.石... Ⅱ.塞... Ⅲ.美术–作品综合集–中国–当代

Ⅳ.J247.5

中国版本图书馆CIP数据核字（2006）第028825号

书　　名	石头·木头·文字
作　　者	塞·格瑞瑟
出　　版	中国文联出版社
发　　行	中国文联出版社发行部
地　　址	北京农展馆南里10号（100026）
经　　销	全国新华书店
责任编辑	王东升
责任印制	王东升
装帧设计	张建荣　杨翠华
印　　刷	云南新闻图片社印刷厂
开　　本	210×230　1/24
字　　数	8千字
印　　张	3.5
印　　数	500册
版　　次	2006年8月第1版第1次印刷
书　　号	ISBN 7-5059-4365-0/I·3400
定　　价	80.00元

本书如有印装质量问题，请直接与承印厂联系

艺 术 家 的 话

艺术，如爱情，是人类一切存在之神圣凝集。人类留下的痕迹有可视或不可视之分，而文字，木头和石头创造出的人物形象，恰好反映出二者之间某种意义上的传承。

我的雕塑和诗歌是形象，它们首要赞美的是造物主的作品—人。好的作品尽其所能在自身内涵的基础上，创造出某些精神的符号，这些符号照亮了一个曾经生活过的生命所留下的不可言喻的超自然印记。次等的作品，不具备超验的特质，充其量不过是些装潢或用来点缀家具的饰品。

我的雕塑的材料大多来自于自然中那些纯净的树木和石头。这些作品被直接雕刻在叫得出名的石头或是任何自然状态形式的材料上。木雕大多是用桉木，相当于欧洲文学作品和歌词里出现的圣树的同义词。艺术表现属于全人类，它早于全球化成为地域特征的时髦名词之前。石头和木头将地球上所有文明都绑在一起，某种意义上是人类艺术尝试和努力的无言的证词。绘画亦然。

我的艺术生涯是一场对创造信仰的考验。通过爱，我们或多或少的接近生命的意义。我的雕塑和诗歌里的意象常常诞生在作品动手之后。它们渐渐演化成一种连贯的感觉，这种感觉便是所谓的内容。当内容有了真实可靠的立足点之后，形式便成了视觉的浓缩。对成功的艺术品而言，内容会被观赏者领略并分享到。我倾其一生的努力就是为了争取赢得那片刻的分享。

我出生于美国马里兰州巴尔的摩市，父亲是俄罗斯人，母亲是罗马尼亚人。他们的上辈人是来自东俄罗斯的农奴。他们对过去的追忆在我生命里留下的是痛苦的经历。在美国成长的犹太人并没有比别的地方的犹太人更不认为自己是另类。我们属于不得不随时躲藏，逃跑，回避社会主流的群体。我父亲送我到一家私立军事院校学习，为的是让我能被社会勉强地接受，而就在那时，我退避到隐秘的世界里，因为在那里我的幸福不至于被认为是一种过分。小小年纪的我就成为了一个保留记忆，保留形象的人。记忆中的这些形象后来都转化成了雕塑和诗歌的象征，与此同时也成了约束它们自己的一种契约。

在 1940 年至 1943 年期间，我就读于马里兰州南部的夏洛特霍尔军事学校(Charlotte Hall Military Academy)。这所有名望的学校建立于 1734 年，是训练外交官和上流社会子弟的场所。后来，移民家庭也送他们的孩子去这所私立学校接受教育。作为首批入学的犹太学生之一，我首当其充地成为当时排犹潮流的冲击对象。学校教育充其量推行的是严格刻板的尚武精神，因为学生们削尖脑袋的想进西点军校—美国军事将才的来源地。艺术指导和诗歌在课程表里是见也见不到的。然而，如俗话所说，学生做好准备，老师自然就到。有这样一位老师，他鼓励我，使我相信自己有丰富的想象力，艺术是将来某一天我应该从事的事业。

高中毕业后，我就学于马里兰州巴尔的摩的约翰霍普金斯大学，进的医学预科班。可是六个星期后，我被开除了，理由是我没有适应环境的能力。才从一个武备环境里出来的我，惊奇地发现，课程表里安排有军事课，却没有艺术，也没有对数学和科学的侧重性。除了学习外，反闪米族人的情绪在学生们中间盛器尘上。

我很艰难地进了宾夕法尼亚州的盖茨堡学院。开课后两星期，我就被排斥在课堂外，问题是犹太人不允许住在学校宿舍内。我勉强上完这学期的课程后，就加入了运送军队和给养的美国商船队。在二战期间，我作为无线电发报员，在各式各样的船舰上航行。战争结束后，我被马里兰大学录取，专业为动物学。1949 年获学士学位。其后，又获英美文学学士学位。二十多年后，取得美国文学和写作的硕士学位。

我守护着永驻在文字和石头里的记忆。作为这样的一名守护人，在我八十岁的今天，能够定位出当年引导我成为雕塑家和诗人的道路。我的祖母茹海尔给我指出了一生所应追寻的道德路线。早年，她成了我生命价值试金石：以爱、善、信这样的顺序来构建生活。

四年的军校生涯奠定了我对政治，战争和仇恨的憎恶。存在于生活方方面面的善与恶两种力量的对抗在此间段已形成，成了我雕刻石头的入门基石。那些年代，我选择了做一名社会和时尚文化的旁观者，此后一生大都保持这样一种状况。

三年在美国商船队的航海经历，使我感受到自然世界里充满了奇观。大海的属性和恐怖形成了我早期诗歌和雕塑里出现的意象，而船舰和水手给予我一个去认识生命意义的微观世界。

马里兰大学的四年间，雕塑并不是我的专业，而在这时期我的艺术和人文教育却进入了全盛时期。听了一堂艺术系的课之后，我再次意识到，我无法适应建立在 19 世纪基础上的教学方式。后来我在一家小规模的学校注册，那里遇到一位黑人雕塑家，威廉·泰勒(William Taylor)[1]。此后的三年内，他一直是我的恩师。他叫我直接在石头，木头和各种材料上雕塑，无需模特或事先构思好的草图作参照。他是位非常直观的大师，仅用眼睛和感觉来创造形象。他热爱雕塑，是他教给了我美学的中心内涵。在那个时代对我们影响大的雕塑家有霍桑·德克里夫特(Jose De Creeft)[2]、威廉·左拉克(William Zorach)[3]、约翰·弗兰拉冈(John Flannagan)[4]、奥思普·扎德金 (Ossip Zadkine)[5]和亨利·莫尔(Henry Moore)[6]。从 1949 年以来，我就一直用石头，木头和文字塑造形象。

亨利·伯恩邦(Henry Birnbaum)是位数学家、诗人、和艺术领域里的年轻天才。他在马里兰大学和乔治华盛顿大学教授英美文学。从马里兰大学一年级起直至我的一生，他都是我的导师。他对我的影响具有某种繁衍性。他引导我认识了哈特·科瑞恩(Hart Crane)[7]、伟大的中国诗人和纽约的艺术生活。他认识阿瑟·克里斯蒂(Arthur Cristy)[8]、阿瑟·威利(Arthur Waley)[9]，这两位早期中国诗的翻译家，以及画家阿瑟·萨皮(Arthur Sappe)[10]。他通晓亚洲哲史，熟悉世界思想界的动态。晚年的亨利成为日本国家科学基金会的负责人。

在 1949 年至 1952 年这段期间，我认识了查尔斯·奥森(Charles Olson)[11]，同他和他的诗，还有华盛顿那帮追随他的诗人们交了朋友。从他这里，我听说到戴南·托马斯(Dylan Thomas)[12] 其人，并拜读了他的诗。从那里，我师从于当代艺术学院的威廉·泰勒，开始了我最初的雕塑课。从这时期始直到 1958 年，均是在弗瑞尔亚洲艺术馆、国家艺术馆及各位伟大的画家、雕塑家和作家的艺术中心度过了所有的午饭时间。

从 1959 年至 1960 年，我被美洲国家组织授予一笔奖金，去墨西哥学习奥尔麦克(Olmec)艺术。这个阶段恐怕对我的艺术创作是最具影响力的一个阶段，因为从这以后，墨西哥的艺术便在我心里落户了，以致墨西哥印第安人的主题至今还我的作品里频频出现。同样地，圣经里有关奇迹和超自然的意象渗透了我的创作思想。墨西哥印第安人的面孔和他们的图案使我着迷，在那里，中国题材的东西比比皆是。奥哈卡(Oaxaca)的印第安人的眼睛绝对是从中国人那里演变来的。据我观察来看，他们雕塑的脸孔与中国的文明有着情感上的联系。在我的作品里，这个观念是最根本的观念，它始终贯穿了我整个创作生涯。在这阶段，我深受一派画家和作家的影响，他们是布朗卡·迪亚兹·德古提锐(Blanca Diez de Guttierez)[13]、波尔提·多明戈·德索尔康(Berte Dominguez de Salkind)[14]、潘丘·多明戈(Poncho Dominguez)[15]。在圣安吉尔(San Angel)，我们举办诗歌朗诵会和画展。就在那里，弗兰西斯科·佐尼嘎(Francisco Zuni-ga)[16] 展出了二十多件他的作品。这一画派里的其他艺术家包括有诗人比尔·瑞乌拉(Bill Rivera)[17]，还有画家霍桑·路易库瓦斯(José Luis Cuevas)[18]，其后来为瑞乌拉的诗集插图。

1965 年，我加入了座落在 56 街的卡佩瑞孔画廊(Capricorn Gallery)。该画廊由画家左伊·阿珀托利兹(Zoé

Apostolides)[19] 资助成立的。在这个自助式的画廊里，我遇见了画家夏洛特·理琪卜罗(Charlotte Lichtblau)[20]。以后的三十多年里，她对我在艺术方面的影响举足轻重。她的艺术观念跨越了几个时代，从艺术的萌芽期，到歌德，一直到德国的表现主义。她的绘画以新、旧约为题材，表达艺术所具有的一种特殊的继承。我将学习到的这个表现形式借鉴到自己的观念中去。她对我的那个影响一直沿袭到今天。

另一位在这时期对我影响最深的是教育家布鲁斯·潘恩(Bruce Payne)[21]，布鲁斯对文学和艺术包罗万象的视野对我未来二十多年的雕塑和诗歌创作奠定了方向。他给予了古典文化遗产一个直接的界面，让人类感情在规定的结构范围内自如地表达出来。

过去的二十多年里，我主要的雕塑对象是石头。最近十年里，我也雕刻木头，主要是浮雕，赞美人类为赎救所作的努力。有一件三联组雕，11 英尺长，7 英尺高，两侧的组雕是红橡木，中间是白杨木，名字叫《哪里有屠杀，哪里就有她》。作品歌颂从纳粹时代的火炉里拯救出生命。我最近的作品是 6 英尺高，7 英尺长的组雕，受噶文·门捷兹(Gavin Menzies)[22] 所写的《1421：中国人发现美洲大陆的那一天》这本书的启发。中国人对生命的认识像一条线始终贯穿我的一生，似乎在这件用桉树木板制作的作品里达到了顶峰。在作品里，史前的和现代的神灵同时存在，女人，男人和小孩形象采用了直接雕塑法。他们的脸孔是由我认识的中西方人拼凑而成的。中国朋友们在中国成长的故事是形成我对人类和人性存在这样一种信仰的新基石。"全球性"并不是一个单纯的地理概念。内涵上讲，人只有一个种类。W·H·奥登(W·H·Auden)[23]，英美诗人，曾和克里斯多夫·伊舍伍德(ChristopherIsherwood)[24] 在 1937 年合写了一个剧本叫《F7 的升华》，里面有一句话："一个人类的意思就是一个人类。我们得学会彼此关爱，否则必死无疑。"

注释

1 威廉·泰勒(William Taylor)1927 年生于华盛顿 D.C.。教授直接雕塑法。创建雕塑家作坊。任教于当代艺术学院、可克仁艺术学院、哥伦比亚特区大学、华盛顿 D.C.的豪沃德大学。

2 霍桑·乔恩德克里夫特(Jose DeCreeft)1884 年生于西班牙的瓜达拉贾拉。当代雕塑家。孩子时就显示出对雕塑的兴趣。1905 年去巴黎学艺，后到纽约教书，对世界上直接雕塑法很有影响。

3 威廉·左拉克(William Zorach)1887 年生于立陶宛。四岁时随家人移民到美国俄亥沃州的克里夫兰。很早时就显示出非凡的艺术才能。曾在克里夫兰艺术学校学习平版画。画过水彩画，在石头上直接雕塑。后到纽约。四十岁上开始在世界上出名。

4 约翰·弗兰拉冈 (John Flannagan)1895 年生于北达科达州的法戈，1942 年死于纽约。在天然石头和其他自然材料上雕刻。30 年代期间活跃于纽约。以石头人像和木雕著名。

5 奥思普·扎德金 (Ossip Zadkine)1890 年生于俄罗斯的斯莫棱斯克，1967 年死于法国巴黎。在巴黎和纽约度过大部分生涯。以立体和表现主义风格的直接雕塑法著称。

6 亨利·莫尔(Henry Moore)生于 1898 年，死于 1886。英国雕塑家。他的雕塑生涯大部分在英国度过，是当代最伟大的直接雕塑家之一。作品有木雕和石雕。

7 哈特·科瑞恩 (Hart Crane)1899 年 7 月生于俄亥沃州的伽里茨威尔，死于 1932 年四月。短寿，酗酒，是 20 年代怒吼一代作家的原型。以反映美国生活的叙事诗《桥》著名。

8 阿瑟·克里斯蒂(Arthur Cristy)中国诗的翻译家和专家。在 30 年代期间，他是少数几个能给学生传达中国诗的含义和美感的学者之一。有关他的资料不多。

9 阿瑟·威利(Arthur Waley)生于 1889 年 8 月 19 日，死于 1966 年 6 月 27 日。著名的英国东方学家和汉学家。

10 阿瑟·萨皮(Arthur Sappe)超现实主义画家。30 至 40 年代住在纽约的东部。有关资料不详。

11 查尔斯·奥森(Charles Olson)生于 1910 年，死于 1970 年。在麻省的沃切斯特长大。在卫斯里央大学和哈佛学习美国文明。成为著名的诗人和思想家。竭力推崇现代诗歌里的古典主义和先锋主义。

12 戴南·托马斯(Dylan Thomas)生于 1914 年 10 月 27 日，死于 1953 年 11 月 9 日。著名的威尔士作家和诗人。

13 布朗卡·迪亚兹·德古提锐(Blanca Diezde Guttierez)一位墨西哥女画家和教育家。生活在墨西哥城和德珀兹兰。

14 波尔提·多明戈·德索尔康(Berte Dominguezde Salkind)墨西哥女剧作家兼诗人。长期居住巴黎。剧本《男巫》于 1962 年在爱尔兰出演。

15 潘丘·多明戈(Poncho Dominguez)墨西哥雕塑家和画家。后期住在巴黎。

16 弗兰西斯科·佐尼嘎(Francisco Zuniga)墨西哥画家。1912 生于科斯塔尼加，死于 1998。主要居住在墨西哥的奥哈卡。属于直接雕塑流派，创作了不少墨西哥纪念雕像。

17 比尔·瑞乌拉(Bill Rivera)墨西哥和美国诗人。后期在马里兰大学任教。

18 霍桑·路易库瓦斯(JoseLuis Cuevas)1993 年生于墨西哥市。自学成材的画家、镌刻师和雕塑家。在 60 年代和 70 年代的拉丁美洲绘画和制版印刷的文艺复兴中起了相当重要的作用。和拉丁美洲的新象征主义运动有关联。

19 左伊·阿珀托利兹(Zoé Apostolides)画家，大部分时间住在纽约。组建了布里奇画廊。死于巴黎。

20 夏洛特·利琪卜罗(Charlotte Lichtblau)生于奥地利维也纳。在纽约度过大部分画家生涯。她的绘画是表现主义形式的绘画，建立与对宗教经历的深刻理解。多次和赛·格瑞塞(Sy Gresser)共同展出作品。

21 布鲁斯·潘恩(Bruce Payne)教育家和演讲家。杜克大学的教授。竭力宣传赛?格瑞塞和夏洛特?利琪卜罗的艺术作品，为他们在大学的画廊里安排了无数的展出。

22 噶文·门捷兹 (Gavin Menzies) 退休的英国皇家海军潜艇指挥官，《1421，中国人发现美洲大陆的那一天》的作者。

23 W·H·奥登(W·H·Auden)1907 年二月生于北约克郡。英国出生的诗人。他的世界观从年轻的叛逆到安格鲁天主教的再发现发展而成。被普遍认为是 20 世纪最伟大的文学界人物之一。1973 年 9 月 28 日逝于维也纳。

24 克里斯多夫·伊舍伍德 (Christopher Isherwood)1904 年 8 月 26 日生于英格兰，1939 年移民美国，居住在加利佛利亚的桑塔莫尼卡直到 1986 年逝世。小说家和剧作家，以《柏林的故事》出名。其书七叔改编成剧本和电影。

Artist's Statement

Art, like love, can be a distillate of all that is holy in human existence. The created human image, in words, wood or stone, reflects a continuity of meaning between the visible and invisible remains of the human imprint.

My sculptures and poems are images. They celebrate the creatures of God - primarily humans. At their best they create within their content the symbols of spirituality that illuminate the unspoken numinous imprint of a lived life. At their worst they fail to have a transcendent quality, and so become decoration, or adornment along with the furniture.

The materials of my sculpture are from nature - raw trees and stones. The sculptures have been carved directly in recognizable stones and naturally occurring materials. Of wood, I carve mostly ash wood - the European equivalent of sacred trees in literature and song. Artistic expression belonged to humankind long before globalization became a popular geographic identification. Stone and wood bind all civilizations on earth, and in a sense are the un-spoken witnesses of human artistic endeavors. Paintings bear the same heritage.

My artistic life is a testament of faith in creativity. Through love, we approach some semblance to meaning. The images in my carvings and poems are often born after beginning a work; then they evolve toward a coherent emotion which can be defined as content. Form is a condensed vision where content has an authentic resting place. When successful, content in an art work becomes visible to a viewer to be shared. That sharing is a moment toward which I have worked all of my life.

I was born in Baltimore Maryland, USA, to a Russian father and Romanian mother. Their parents came from eastern Russia and were farm serfs. The memory of their narrated experiences left a rather bitter imprint on my life. Growing up Jewish in America did not diminish that feeling of being other, of belonging to a group that has to hide, run and disassociate from the mainstream of society. By the time I was sent to a private military school to become more acceptable to society, I had retreated to a private world where my happiness dwelled without impositions. I became a keeper of memory, of image, at a very early age. The guardians of memory became symbols for the carvings and poems, and

too, their indentures.

I attended Charlotte Hall Military Academy in southern Maryland, 1940-1943. This prestigious high school was established in 1734. It was a proving ground for diplomats' children and other upper echelon families. Immigrant families later were to send their children for this private education. One of the first Jews ever to be accepted in this institution, I was subjected to the usual anti-semitism fashionable at that time. The education at best was rigid with militarism since many of the attendees were striving to be accepted at West Point - one source of American's military leaders. Art instruction and poetry were absent in the curricula but as always, when the student is ready the teacher appears. One such teacher gave me the inspiration to believe that I had a very good imagination, and that I should someday pursue art.

After high school graduation I attended Johns Hopkins University in Baltimore, Maryland, majoring in pre-medical studies. I was expelled after six weeks because of an inability to adjust to the environment. Having come from a military environment, I was stunned to find that the curriculum contained courses for the military, no studies in art, and special emphasis on mathematics and sciences. Incidental to the studies, anti-semitism was standard fare within the student body.

With great difficulty, I then enrolled in Gettysburg College, Gettysburg, Pennsylvania where I was ostracized two weeks after opening classes. The problem was that Jews were not allowed to sleep in the housing provided by the school. I managed to finish the semester and then enlisted in the US Merchant Marine carrying war supplies to the troops. I sailed on numerous vessels as a Radio Operator for the duration of World War II. After the war, I enrolled in Maryland University and received a Bachelor of Science degree in 1949, majoring in Zoological Sciences. I later received an equivalent BA in English and American Literature. And decades later, an M.A. in American Literature and Creative Writing.

As a keeper of memory in images and words, I can now at age 80 pinpoint the path that led me to become a sculptor and poet. My grandmother Ruchel gave me a sense of ethical pathways to follow in life. From a very early age, she became a touchstone for human values: life was structured with love, goodness and faith, in that order.

My attendance at military school for four years shaped my distaste for politics, war, and hate. The opposing forces of good and evil that attend all human lives, formed at this time, became the basis of my approach to carving stones. Out of these years, I became by choice an outsider to the society and to popular culture. I have remained so most of my life.

Three years at sea in the US Merchant Marines gave me a sense of wonder that pervaded the natural world. The sea and its attributes and terrors shaped much of the imagery of my early poems and sculptures. The ships and its sailors gave me a microcosmic view of what it meant to be human.

At the University of Maryland for four years, my education in the arts and culture bloomed, although I did not study sculpture at the University. Again, after hearing one lecture from the art department, I realized I could not conform to the requirements that were based on 19th century teaching. I enrolled in a small school where a black sculptor, William Taylor[1], became my mentor for the next three years. He taught me to carve in stone, wood and other materials directly, without any model for guidance, or drawings for preconceived ideas. He was a visual master using only his eyes and sensibilities to create images. He loved carving and taught me the internal functioning of aesthetics. Our influences at that time were the great carvers Jose DeCreeft[2], William Zorach[3], John Flannagan[4], Ossip Zadkine[5], and Henry Moore[6]. From that time on, 1949, I have carved stone, wood and words.

Henry Birnbaum was a mathematician, poet and young genius in the field of art. He taught English and American literature at the University of Maryland and George Washington University. He was my teacher from my first year at Maryland and throughout my life. His influence was seminal. He introduced me to the poet Hart Crane[7], the great Chinese poets, and the artistic life of New York City. He knew Arthur Cristy[8], Arthur Waley[9], early translators of Chinese poetry, the painter Arthur Sappé[10]; he was thoroughly familiar with Asian philosophy and perceptions of the world. Later in life he was head of the National Science Foundation's Center in Japan.

During the period 1949-1952, I became friends with Charles Olson[11], his poetry and the poets who were his disciples in Washington DC. It was here I heard Dylan Thomas[12] read his poems, and where I attended my first sculpture classes under William Taylor at the Institute of Contemporary Arts. During this time through 1958, daily lunch times were spent at the Freer Gallery of Asian Art, the National Art Gallery and other centers of great painters, sculptors and writers.

In 1959-60, I received a grant from the Organization of American States to study Olmec art in Mexico. This period was perhaps one of the most influential since the art of Mexico from that period has remained with me; motifs still appear in my sculptures as consistently as Biblical imagery pervades my concept of the miraculous and the transcendent. The faces of Mexican Indians fascinated me, as well as their designs. Chinese motifs appeared everywhere, and the eyes of many Indians in the Oaxaca area were surely derived from Chinese people. In their sculptures, the faces were emotionally linked to the Chinese civilization within my perception. Within my carving, this idea became seminal and has remained so throughout my carving life. I was also strongly influenced at this time by a family of painters and writers : Blanca Diez de Guttierez[13] , Berte Dominguez de Salkind[14], and Poncho Dominguez[15]. In San Angel, we held poetry readings and art exhibitions. It was here that

Francisco Zuniga[16] exhibited 20 of his drawings. Other artists in the group included Bill Rivera[17], a poet, and José Luis Cuevas[18], a painter who later illustrated his book of poems.

In 1965, I joined the Capricorn Gallery on 56th Street, founded by the painter Zoé Apostolides.[19] In this cooperative gallery, I met the painter Charlotte Lichtblau[20]. For the next three decades her influence became important to my work. Her artistic vision spanned the beginnings of art through the Gothic into German expressionism. Her paintings, based on the Old and New Testaments, represented a specific continuity from which I learned and incorporated into my own vision. That influence persists today.

Another seminal influence at this time was the educator Bruce Payne[21] whose encompassing views of literature and art helped shape the direction my sculptures and poems were to take in the forthcoming decades. He gave the classical heritage an immediacy that permitted human feelings to be freely expressed within the confines of invented structure.

During the past two decades I have carved primarily in stone . Over the past ten years, I have been carving wood, mostly bas relief, celebrating a humanity struggling for redemption.

One wooden panel 11 feet long, 7 feet high, is a triptych. The two side panels are red oak; the center panel is tulip poplar. The work, Where The Slain Are, There Is She, celebrates the retrieval of life from the ovens of the Nazi era. My last work, a panel 6 feet high, 7 feet long, was inspired by a book, 1421, The Day the Chinese Discovered America by Gavin Menzies[22]. The Chinese perception of being has been a thread throughout my life and seems to have culminated in this current work, carved in planks of ash wood. The Gods of prehistory and history are present. Women, men and children pervade the directly carved wood. The faces are pastiches of Chinese and Western people I now know, and whose narration of growing up in China has formed a new bedrock of faith in the human presence. Global is not geographic imposition of idea. Within, people are one. As W. H. Auden[23], the American/British poet wrote with Christopher Isherwood[24] in The Ascent of F7 in 1937: one means just what it implies. 'we will learn to love each other or die.'

1 William Taylor. Born in Washington, D.C., 1927, teacher of direct carving sculpture. Founded Sculptors Studio, Washington, D.C. Taught at Institute of Contemporary Art, Corcoran School of Art, University of District of Columbia, and Howard University, Washington, D.C.

2 Jose DeCreeft. Born in Guadalajara, Spain in 1884, modernist sculptor. Interested in sculpture as a child. Studied in Paris in 1905. Taught in New York City and became a global influence for direct carving in stone.

3 William Zorach. Born in 1887 in Lithuania. Immigrated with his family to the United States at the age of four, settling in Cleveland, Ohio. Zorach displayed an exceptional artistic talent at a young age and began studying lithography at night at the Cleveland School of Art. Painted watercolors, then began carving directly in stone. Came to New York and became world famous in the late forties.

4 John Flannagan. Born in 1895, Fargo, North Dakota, died in 1942, New York, New York. Carved field stones and other natural materials. Was active in New York in the late 30's. Was best known for stone figure sculpture and wood carving.

5 Ossip Zadkine. Born in Smolensk, Russia, 1890, died in Paris, France, 1967. Spent most of his career in Paris and New York. Often known for direct sculptures carved in cubistic and expressionistic styles.

6 Henry Moore. Born in 1898, died in 1986. British sculptor. Lived most of professional life in the United Kingdom. Became one of the greatest contemporary direct carvers, in wood and stone.

7 Hart Crane. Born in Garrettsville, Ohio, July, 1899, died on 27 April 1932. Short-lived and hard-drinking, an archetype of the Roaring Twenties author. Best known as poet of The Bridge (1930), an epic vision of American life.

8 Arthur Cristy. Translator and scholar of Chinese poetry. For students in America during the 1930's, he was one of the few scholars who could give students a sense of the nuances and beauty of Chinese poetry. Little information about him is available.

9 Arthur Waley. Born on August 19, 1889, died on June 27, 1966, a noted English orientalist and sinologist.

10 Arthur Sappe. Surrealistic painter who lived on the lower East Side of New York City during the 30's and 40's. Information about him is not available.

11 Charles Olson . Born in 1910, died in 1970. Raised in Worcester, Massachusetts, and educated at Wesleyan University and Harvard, where he studied American civilization. He became a famous poet and thinker, proselytizing the classics as well as the avant garde in modern poetry.

12 Dylan Thomas. Born on October 27, 1914, died November 9, 1953, a famous Welsh poet and writer.

13 Blanca Diez de Guttierez. A Mexican woman educator and painter. Lived in Mexico, DF and Tepotzlan.

14 Berte Dominguez de Salkind. Playwright and poet from Mexico. Spent her life in Paris. The Warlock, a play, was produced in Ireland around 1962.

15 Poncho Dominguez. Mexican sculptor and painter. Spent latter part of his life in Paris.

16 Francisco or Paco Zuniga. Mexican painter. Born in Costa Rica, 1912, died in 1998. Spent life in Mexico, particularly Oaxaca. Direct carver and also made monumental figures of Mexican archetypes.

17 Bill Rivera. Mexican-American poet. Later taught at the University of Maryland.

18 José Luis Cuevas. Born in Mexico City in 1933. A self-taught drawer, engraver and sculptor. Played a pivotal role in Latin America's drawing and printmaking renaissance of the sixties and seventies. Also associated with Latin America's neofigurative movement.

19 Zoé Apostolides. Painter, worked in New York City most of her life. Founded Bridge Gallery. Died in Paris.

20 Charlotte Lichtblau. Born in Vienna, Austria, painted most of her life in New York City. Her paintings are expressionistic, based always on a profound understanding of the nature of religious experience. Exhibited widely with the sculptor Sy Gresser.

21 Bruce Payne. Educator and lecturer. Professor at Duke University for several decades, he advocated the art works of Sy Gresser and Charlotte Lichtblau by arranging exhibits at numerous university galleries.

22 Gavin Menzies. Retired Royal Navy Submarine Commanding Officer, author of 1421, The Day The Chinese Discovered America.

23 W. H. Auden (Wystan Hugh Auden). Born in York, North Yorkshire, in February 1907. English-born poet, whose world view developed from youthful rebellion to rediscovered Anglo-Catholicism. He is widely viewed as one of the greatest literary figures of the 20th century. Died 28 September, 1973, in Vienna.

24 Christopher Isherwood. Born in England on August 26, 1904, emigrated to the U.S. in 1939 and lived in Santa Monica California until his death in 1986. Novelist and playwright, best known for The Berlin Stories, adapted as the play and film.

目 录
Table of Contents

木头(Wood)

文字(Words)

石 头
Stone

陈列在美国驻塞内加尔首都达喀尔的大使馆的一组雕塑。

A group of statues displayed at the American Embassy, Dakar, Senegal.

（左）作品名称：面孔——对西蒙的敬意。尺寸（英寸）：8"x10"x13"。材料：石灰石。创作期：1967。

(Left) Title: Faces: Homage to Simon. Size: 8"x10"x13". Material: Limestone. Year: 1967.

（中）作品名称：花环。尺寸（英寸）：12"x9"x13"。材料：石灰石。创作期：1967。

(Middle) Title: Wreath. Size: 12"x9"x13". Material: Limestone. Year: 1967.

（右）作品名称：人体风景。尺寸（英寸）：12"x8"x10"。材料：石灰石。创作期：1967。

(Right) Title: Human Landscape. Size: 12"x8"x10". Material: Limestone. Year: 1967.

作品名称:天使的集聚。尺寸（英寸）:30"x16"x12"。材料:冻石。
创作期:1998。作为伯斯埃尔犹太教堂的永久收藏品陈列在弗吉尼亚州,阿灵顿的犹太大屠杀祈祷圣址。

Title: A Gathering of Angels I. Size: 30"x16"x12". Material: Steatite.
Year: 1998. Displayed at the Holocaust Prayer Site, permanent collection of Beth El Synagogue, Arlington, Virginia.

作品名称:克图拉

尺寸（英寸）:15"x 13"x 45"

材料:石灰石

创作期:1985

陈列在纽约州纽约市的圣·约翰大教堂

Title: Keturah.

Size: 15"x 13"x 45".

Material: Limestone.

Year: 1985.

 Displayed at the Cathedral Church of St. John the Divine, New York City, N.Y.

作品名称:见证人(浮雕)。尺寸（英寸）:24"x4"x38"。

材料:德克萨斯石灰石。创作期:1985。

陈列在纽约州纽约市的圣·约翰大教堂。

Title: The Witnesses (Bas Relief). Size: 24"x4"x38".

Material: Texas Limestone. Year: 1985.

Displayed at the Cathedral Church of St. John the Divine, New York City, N.Y.

作品名称:一乘一
尺寸(英寸):10"x 8"x 16"
材料:白色大理石
创作期:1967
陈列在康奈狄克州耶鲁大学校园内

Title: One x One.
Size: 10"x 8"x 16".
Material: White Marble.
Year: 1967.
Displayed at Yale University Campus,
New Haven, Connecticut.

作品名称:归属
尺寸(英寸):24" x8" x26"
材料:佛蒙特大理石
创作期:1994

Title: Belonging.
Size: 24" x8" x26"
Material: Vermont marble.
Year: 1994.

作品名称:亚伯拉翰和海格尔

尺寸(英寸):16" x13" x41"

材料:石灰石

创作期:1984

Title: Abraham and Hagar .

Size: 16" x13" x41" .

Material: Limestone.

Year: 1984.

作品名称：圣·富兰西斯的梦
尺寸（英寸）：28" x15" x67"
材料：白色大理石
创作期：1975-1985

Title: Dreams of St. Francis.
Size: 28" x15" x67".
Material: White Marble.
Year: 1975-85.

作品名称:养育。尺寸(英寸):12"x12"x10"。材料:田纳西粉色大理石。创作期:1996

Title: Nurture. Size: 12"x12"x10". Material: Tennessee Pink Marble. Year: 1996.

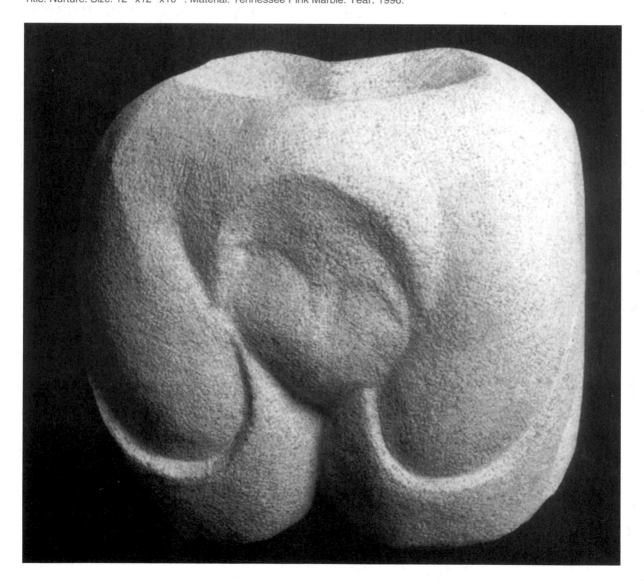

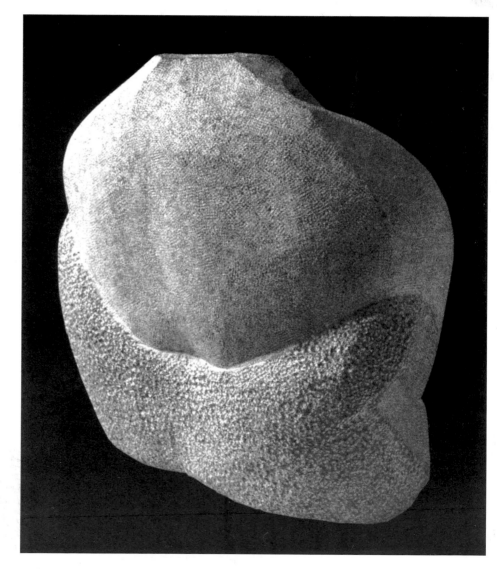

作品名称:鸟翼中的女人
尺寸（英寸）:14"x8"x12"
材料:冻石
创作期:1994

Title: Woman in Bird's Wings.
Size: 14"x8"x12".
Material: Steatite.
Year: 1994.

作品名称：从十字架上放下的耶稣。尺寸（英寸）：14"x16"x15"。材料：石灰石。创作期：1983

Title: Deposition. Size: 14"x16"x15". Material: Limestone. Year: 1983.

作品名称：广岛的天使

尺寸（英寸）：12"x14"x29"

材料：冻石

创作期：1992

Title: Hiroshima's Angel.

Size: 12"x14"x29".

Material: Steatite.

Year: 1992.

作品名称:救援。尺寸(英寸):14"x12"x12"。材料:田纳西粉色大理石。创作期:1984。

Title: Rescue. Size: 14"x12"x12". Material: Tennessee Pink Marble. Year: 1984.

作品名称:广岛之五
尺寸(英寸):30"x18"x17"
材料:印第安娜石灰石
创作期:1978

Title: Hiroshima V.
Size: 30"x18"x17".
Material: Indiana Limestone.
Year: 1978.

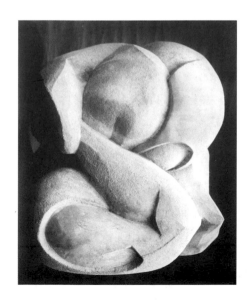

作品名称:爱抚。尺寸（英寸）:21"x13"x12"。材料:田纳西粉色大理石。创作期:1994。

Title: Caress. Size: 21"x13"x12". Material: Tennessee Pink Marble. Year: 1994.

作品名称:品托。尺寸(英寸):8"x7"x15"。
材料:田纳西粉色大理石。创作期:1962。

Title: Pinto. Size: 8"x7"x15".
Material: Tennessee Pink Marble. Year: 1962.

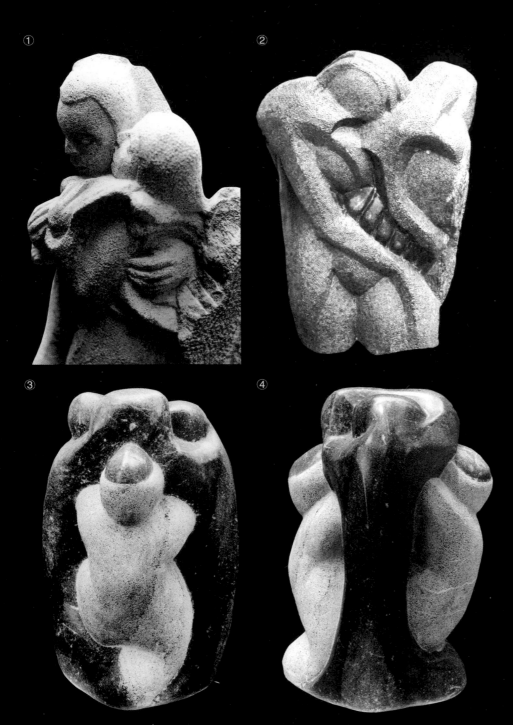

① 作品名称:誓约
尺寸（英寸）:10"x8"x11"
材料:石灰石
创作期:1988

Title: Vow .
Size: 10" x8" x11."
Material: Limestone.
Year: 1988.

② 作品名称:契约
尺寸（英寸）:13"x9"x11"
材料:冻石
创作期:1995

Title: The Bond.
Size: 13" x9" x11."
Material: Steatite.
Year: 1995.

③④ 作品名称:我－你之十二
尺寸（英寸）:12"x12"x24"
材料:田纳西粉色大理石
创作期:1983

Title: I–Thou XII.
Size: 12" x12" x24" .
Material: Tennessee Pink Marble.
Year: 1983.

作品名称:特拉克派克
尺寸（英寸）:8"x12"x18"
材料:沙卵石
创作期:1961

Title: Tlacopac.
Size: 8"x12"x18".
Material: Sandstone Pebble.
Year: 1961.

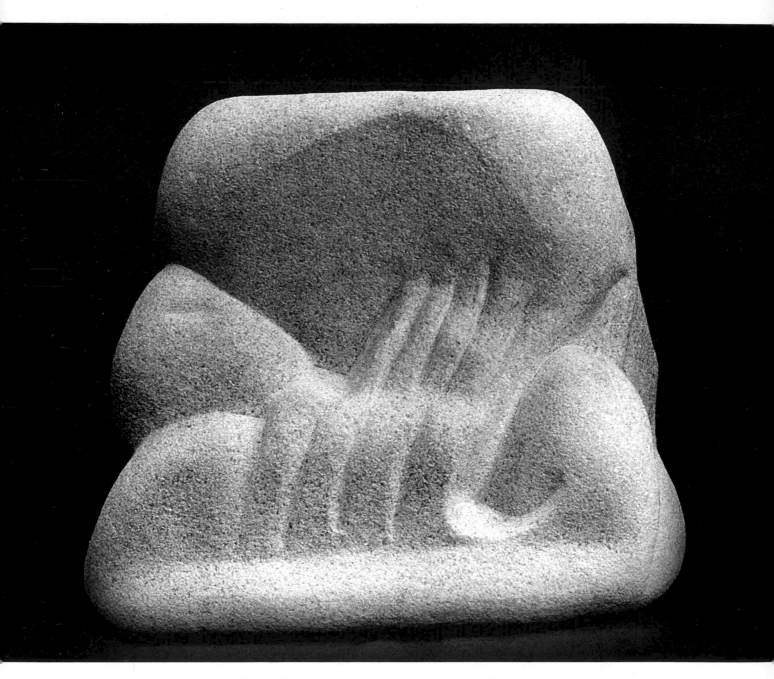

作品名称:温柔（你－我之三）。尺寸（英寸）:13"x7"x9"。材料:佛蒙特白色大理石。创作期:1981。

Title: Tenderness (I–Thou III). Size: 13"x7"x9." Material: Vermont White Marble. Year: 1981.

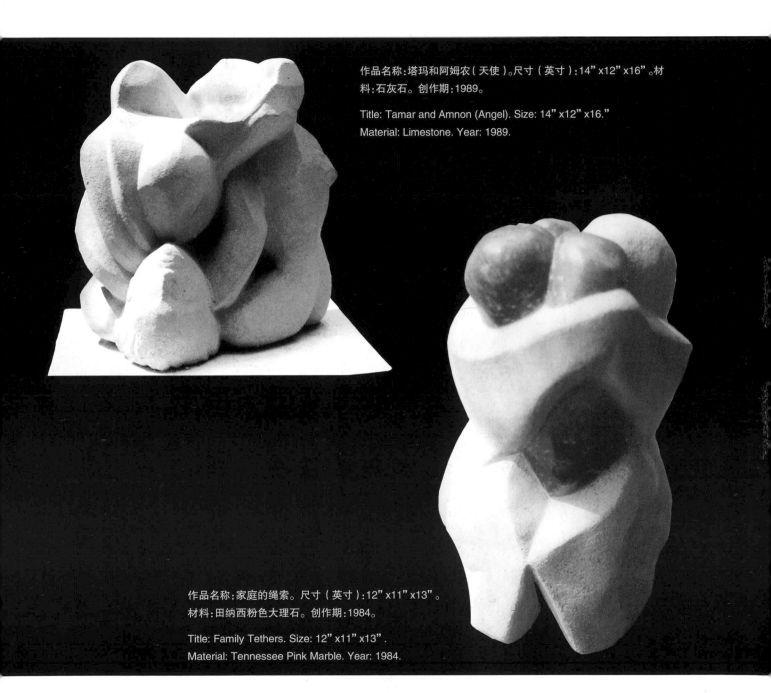

作品名称:塔玛和阿姆农(天使)。尺寸(英寸):14"x12"x16"。材料:石灰石。创作期:1989。

Title: Tamar and Amnon (Angel). Size: 14" x12" x16."
Material: Limestone. Year: 1989.

作品名称:家庭的绳索。尺寸(英寸):12"x11"x13"。
材料:田纳西粉色大理石。创作期:1984。

Title: Family Tethers. Size: 12" x11" x13".
Material: Tennessee Pink Marble. Year: 1984.

作品名称：麦克。尺寸（英寸）：12"x9"x14"。材料：明尼苏达红色花岗岩。创作期：1960。

Title: Michael. Size: 12"x9"x14". Material: Minnesota Red Granite. Year: 1960.

作品名称：戴尔的头像。尺寸（英寸）：14"x12"x14"。材料：石灰石。创作期：2005。

Title: Portrait of Del. Size: 14"x12"x14". Material: Limestone. Year: 2005.

①

②

③

① 作品名称：夫妻。尺寸（英寸）：14"x10"x13"。
材料：白色大理石。创作期：1981。

Title: Couple. Size: 14"x10"x13".
Material: White Marble. Year: 1981.

② 作品名称：土生土长的妇女。尺寸（英寸）：12"x10"x12"。
材料：田纳西粉色大理石。创作期：2005。

Title: Indigenous Woman. Size: 12"x10"x12".
Material: Tennessee Pink Marble. Year: 2005.

③ 作品名称：试金石（浮雕）。尺寸（英寸）：24"x3"x28"。
材料：冻石。创作期：2000。

Title: Touchstones (Bas Relief). Size: 24"x3"x28".
Material: Steatite. Year: 2000.

作品名称:克图拉

尺寸（英寸）:15"x13"x45"

材料:石灰石

创作期:1985

Title: Keturah.

Size: 15" x13" x45" .

Material: Limestone.

Year: 1985.

作品名称:爱娃。尺寸（英寸）:10"x7"x12"。
材料:白色大理石。创作期:1951。

Title: Eve. Size: 10" x7" x12".
 Material: White Marble. Year: 1951.

① 作品名称:广岛之四
尺寸（英寸）:25"x 13"x 21"
材料:石灰石
创作期:1983
弗吉尼亚州的 Del Lewis 的私人收藏

Title: Hiroshima IV.
Size: 25"x 13"x 21."
Material: Limestone.
Year: 1983.
Collection of Del Lewis, McLean, Virginia.

② 作品名称:我和你之五
尺寸（英寸）:14"x 12"x 25"
材料:石灰石
创作期:1981
由华盛顿 D.C. 犹太教父 Harold White 收藏

Title: I–Thou V.
Size: 14"x 12"x 25".
Material: Limestone.
Year: 1981.
Collection of Rabbi Harold White, Washington, D.C.

③ 作品名称:城市风景
尺寸（英寸）:24"x 9"x 38"
材料:大理石
创作期:1979

Title: Cityscape.
Size: 24"x 9"x 38."
Material: Marble.
Year: 1979.

④ 作品名称:舞蹈者
尺寸（英寸）:26"x 8"x 30"
材料:佛蒙特白色大理石
创作期:1978

Title: The Dancers.
Size: 26"x 8"x 30."
Material: Vermont White Marble.
Year: 1978.

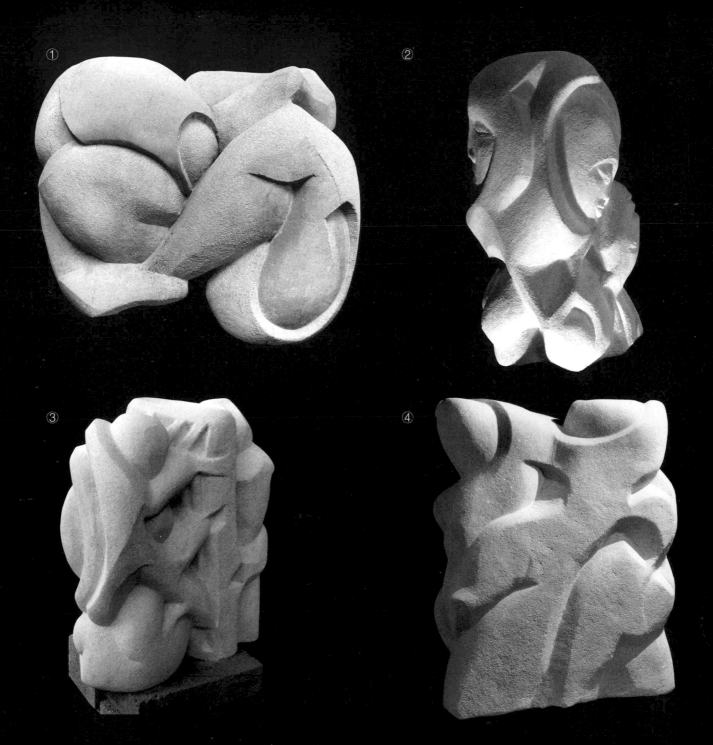

③ 作品名称:挣扎。尺寸(英寸):12"x 9"x 26"。材料:白色大理石。创作期:1954。
Title: Struggle (Back view). Size: 12"x 9"x 26".Material: White Marble. Year: 1954.

④ 作品名称:拥抱。尺寸(英寸):18"x 15"x 22"。材料:石灰石。创作期:1959。
Title: Embrace. Size: 18"x 15"x 22". Material: Limestone. Year: 1959.

⑤ 作品名称:活着(之二)。(英寸):16"x 9"x11" 。材料:佛吉尼亚绿岩。创作期:1981。
Title: Alive II. Size: 16"x 9"x 11" Material: Virginia Greenstone. Year: 1981.

⑥ 作品名称:梦见成型。(英寸):14"x8"x28"。材料:白色大理石。创作期:1987。
Title: Dream of Becoming. Size: 14"x8"x28". Material: White Marble. Year: 1987.

⑦ 作品名称:塞拉和海格尔。尺寸(英寸):16"x13"x46"。材料:石灰石。创作期:1986。
Title: Sarai and Hagar. Size: 16"x13"x46" . Material: Limestone. Year: 1986.

①

②

① 作品名称:神圣家庭之二
尺寸(英寸):18"x 5"x 45"
材料:石灰石
创作期:1988

Title: Holy Family II .
Size: 18"x 5"x 45".
Material: Limestone.
Year: 1988.

② 作品名称:阿布瑞若
尺寸(英寸):12"x 14"x 28"
材料:佛蒙特白色大理石
创作期:1980

Title: Abrazo.
Size: 12"x 14"x 28."
Material: Vermont White Marble.
Year: 1980.

③ 作品名称：广岛之恋之三。尺寸（英寸）：27"x 15"x 10"。材料：冻石。创作期：1975。
Title: Hiroshima Mon Amore III. Size: 27"x 15"x 10". Material: Steatite. Year: 1975.

④ 作品名称：船上恋人。尺寸（英寸）：18"x 7"x 28"。材料：白色大理石。创作期：1981。
Title: Boat Lovers. Size: 18"x 7"x 28". Material: White Marble. Year: 1981.

⑤ 作品名称：天使的集会。尺寸（英寸）：33"x13"x23"。材料：冻石。创作期：1991。
Title: Gathering of Angels. Size: 33"x13"x23." Material: Steatite. Year: 1991.

⑥ 作品名称：康斯坦扎和鸟。（英寸）：14"x 10"x12"。材料：田纳西粉色大理石。创作期：1980。
Title: Constanza Among Birds. Size: 14"x 10"x12." Material: Tennessee Pink Marble. Year: 1980.

⑦ 作品名称：生命的气息。尺寸（英寸）：12"x16"x24"。材料：白色大理石。创作期：1981。
Title: Breath of Life. Size: 12"x16"x24". Material: White Marble. Year: 1981.

①

②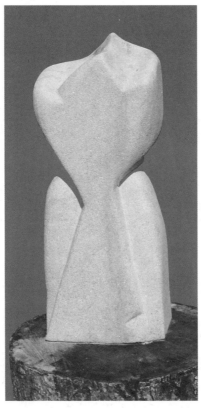

① 作品名称：那西缅托（新生儿）
尺寸（英寸）：17"x 14"x 60"
材料：佛蒙特大理石
创作期：1967–69

Title: Nacimiento.
Size: 17"x 14"x 60".
Material: Vermont Marble.
Year: 1967–69.

② 作品名称：瀑布里的女人
（英寸）：14"x6"x31"
材料：白色大理石
创作期：1965

Title: Woman in a Waterfall.
Size: 14"x6"x31".
Material: White Marble.
Year: 1965.

① ② ③

④ ⑤ ⑥

42

① 作品名称：危地马拉来的女人。尺寸（英寸）:13"x 10"x 16"。材料:冻石。创作期:1994。纽约市 " 气 " 画廊的收藏品。
Title: Woman from Guatemala. Size: 13"x 10"x 16". Material: Steatite. Year: 1994. Collection of Chi Gallery, New York City, N.Y.

② 作品名称：带鸟的男孩。（英寸）:13"x15"x19"。材料:黑色花岗岩。创作期:1957。
Title: Boy with Bird. Size: 13"x15"x19". Material: Black Granite. Year: 1957.

③ 作品名称：小熊。尺寸（英寸）:11"x10"x14"。材料:冻石。创作期:2002。
Title: Little Bear. Size: 11"x10"x14". Material: Steatite. Year: 2002.

④ 作品名称：吉尔头像。尺寸:真人大小。材料:石灰石。创作期:1972。
Title: Head of Jill. Size: Life Size. Material: Limestone. Year: 1972.

⑤ 作品名称：普罗米修斯。尺寸（英寸）:30"x19"x14"。材料:沙石。创作期:1950。
Title: Prometheus. Size: 30"x19"x14". Material: Sandstone Boulder. Year: 1950.

⑥ 作品名称：梦境。尺寸（英寸）:16"x13"x46"。材料:石灰石。创作期:1979。
Title: Dreams. Size: 14"x12"x26". Material: Limestone. Year: 1979.

作品名称：面具。尺寸（英寸）:27"x9"x13"。材料:冻石。创作期:2002。

Title: Masks. Size: 27"x9"x13". Material: Steatite. Year: 2002.

作品名称:记忆的持续(浮雕)

尺寸(英寸):23"x3"x32"

材料:意大利白色大理石

创作期:2003

Title: Persistenceo (Bas Relief).

Size: 23" x3" x32" .

Material: Italian White Marble.

Year: 2003.

作品名称:最后的晚餐,又名人性之二 (浮雕)。尺寸(英寸):65"x5"x36"。材料:德克萨斯石灰石。创作期:1986

Title: Last Supper or Humanity II (Bas Relief). Size: 65"x5"x36". Material: Texas Limestone. Year: 1986.

作品名称:见证人 (浮雕)

尺寸（英寸）:24"x4"x38"

材料:德克萨斯石灰石

创作期:1985

Title: The Witnesses (Bas Relief).

Size: 24" x4" x38".

Material: Texas Limestone.

Year: 1985.

作品名称:亚伯拉翰和海格尔(浮雕)。尺寸（英寸）:24"x38"x4"。
材料:德克萨斯石灰石。创作期:1986。

Title: Abraham and Hagar (Bas relief). Size: 24" x38" x4".
Material: Texas Limestone. Year: 1986.

作品名称:记忆的持续（浮雕）。尺寸（英寸）:21"x2"x30"。
材料:意大利白色大理石。创作期:2003。

Title: Persistence of Memory (Bas Relief). Size: 21" x2" x30".
Material: Italian White Marble. Year: 2003.

作品名称:亚伯拉翰和伊萨克(浮雕)。尺寸（英寸）:20"x15"x21"。材料:石灰石。创作期:1977。

Title: Abraham and Isaac (Bas Relief). Size: 20"x15"x21". Material: Limestone. Year: 1977.

作品名称：阿麦农和塔玛（浮雕）。尺寸（英寸）：24"x4"x26"。材料：德克萨斯石灰石。创作期：1989。

Title: Amnon and Tamar (Bas Relief). Size: 24" x4" x26". Material: Texas Limestone. Year: 1989.

木 头
Wood

作品名称：最后的家庭(局部)。尺寸（英寸）：28"x20"x50"。材料：桉木。创作期：1974。

Title: Last Family(Detail). Size: 28"x20"x50". Material: Ash Wood. Year: 1974.

①

①作品名称:母亲和孩子
尺寸（英寸）:36"x19"x 19"
材料:白杨木
创作期:1967–77
1980 年在安提澳克学院展出

Title: Mother & Child.
Size: 36"x19"x 19".
Material: Tulip Poplar.
Year: 1967–77.
Antioch College Exhibit, 1980.

②作品名称:孩子们的监护者
尺寸（英寸）:27"x 20"x 55"
材料:杉木
创作期:1967

Title: Guardian for Children.
Size: 27"x 20"x 55".
Material: Cedar Wood.
Year: 1967.

②

③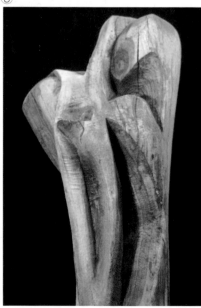

③作品名称:将耶稣从十字架上放下来
尺寸（英寸）:16"x 12"x 30"
材料:黑核桃木
创作期:1971

Title: Deposition.
Size:16"x 12"x 30".
Material: Black Walnut.
Year: 1971.

作品名称:最后的家庭
尺寸(英寸):28"x 20"x 50"
材料:桉木
创作期:1974

Title: Last Family.
Size: 28"x 20"x 50".
Material: Ash Wood.
Year: 1974.

作品名称：品托 之二。（英寸）：8"x8"x15"。
材料：杉木。创作期：1962。

Title: Pinto II. Size: 8"x8"x15".
Material: Cedar Wood. Year: 1962.

作品名称：缠绵的结束。尺寸（英寸）：13"x17"x18"。
材料：绿色斯盖勒石。创作期：1999。

Title: Obsession's End. Size: 13"x17"x18".
Material: Green Schuyler Stone. Year: 1999.

作品名称：哪里有屠杀，哪里就有她（三联版的局部）。（英寸）：132"x14"x72"。材料：白杨木。创作期：2004。

Title: Where the Slain Are, There Is She (Detail of Triptych Center Panel). Size: 132"x14"x72". Material: Tulip Poplar Wood. Year: 2004.

①

①作品名称:哪里有屠杀,哪里就有她（三联版的局部）
（英寸）:132"x14"x72"
材料:白杨木
创作期:2004

Title: Where the Slain Are, There Is She (Detail of Triptych Center Panel). Size: 132" x14" x72".
Material: Tulip Poplar Wood.
Year: 2004.

②作品名称:乔纳的梦(局部)
（英寸）:60"x4"x40"
材料:桉木
创作期:2003

Title: Jonah's Dream (Detail).
Size: 60" x4" x40".
Material: Ash Wood.
Year: 2003.

②

③

③作品名称:乔纳的梦
（英寸）:60"x4"x40"
材料:桉木
创作期:2003

Title: Jonah's Dream .
Size: 60" x4" x40".
Material: Ash Wood.
Year: 2003.

1973年陈列在纽约市博尼维画廊的木雕。同时展出的有 Charlotte Lichtblau 的油画。
Wood Sculpture exhibited together with Charlotte Lichtblau's paintings at Benevy Gallery, New York, NY, 1973

(左) 作品名称:神圣的一对 。尺寸 (英寸):14"x 17"x 48"。材料:杉木。创作期:1970。
(Left) Title: Holy Couple. Size: 14"x 17"x 48". Material: Cedar Wood. Year: 1970.

(右) 作品名称:给大卫涂油 。尺寸 (英寸):15"x 18"x 72"。材料:桉木。创作期:1971。
(Right) Title: Anointment of David. Size: 15"x 18"x 72". Material: Ash Wood. Year: 1971.

作品名称:柏木的麦丹娜
尺寸(英寸):14"x16"x30"
材料:柏木
创作期:1984

Title: Juniper Madonna.
Size: 14"x16"x30".
Material: Juniper Wood.
Year: 1984.

作品名称：这世界曾属于我

尺寸（英寸）：24"x 22"x 48"

材料：梓木

创作期：1955

Title: This World Was Mine.

Size: 24"x 22"x 48".

Material: Catalpa.

Year: 1955.

作品名称:垂死的鸟 。尺寸（英寸）:15"x 12"x 48"。
材料:黑核桃木。创作期:1973。

Title: Dying Bird. Size: 15"x 12"x 48".
Material: Black Walnut. Year: 1973.

作品名称:家庭 。尺寸（英寸）:27"x 17"x 60"。
材料:槐木。创作期:1963。

Title: The Family.Size: 27"x 17"x 60".
Material: Locust Wood. Year: 1963.

作品名称:婚礼 。尺寸(英寸):17"x 15"x 46"。
材料:杉木。创作期:1972。
1975 年在康纳狄克州耶鲁大学伯克利中心展出。

Title: The Wedding. Size: 17"x 15"x 46".
Material: Cedar Wood. Year: 1972.
Exhibited at Berkeley Center at Yale Divinity School, Connecticut, 1972.

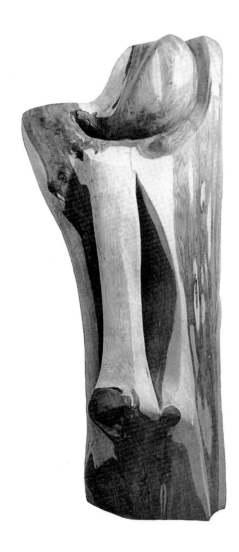

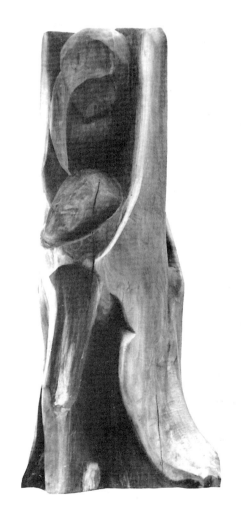

作品名称:大海来的麦丹娜 。尺寸(英寸):19"x 13"x 44"。
材料:黑核桃木。创作期:1973。
1975 年在康纳狄克州耶鲁大学伯克利中心展出。

Title: Madonna from the Sea. Size: 19"x 13"x 44".
Material: Black Walnut. Year: 1973.
Exhibited at Berkeley Center at Yale Divinity School, Connecticut, 1975.

作品名称:麦丹娜再生。尺寸（英尺）:6'x20"。
材料:黑胡桃木。创作期:1972。
陈列在美国驻塞内加尔首都达喀尔的大使馆。

Title: Madonne Reborn. Size: 6'x20".
Material: Black Walnut Wood. Year: 1972.
Displayed at the American Embassy, Dakar, Senegal.

作品名称:哺食者
尺寸（英寸）:15"x 14"x 44"
材料:核桃木
创作期:1976

Title: The Feeders.
15"x 14"x 44".
Material: Walnut Wood.
Year: 1976.

文 字

Words

三个记忆

1.

苦涩的骨头，蜜甜的骨髓所在地，
浅浅的根，深埋的种子会苏醒。
承诺是心脏与痛苦的锁链
风景以自身的秘密
与之连成一线。
彼此都承认
与地球初雨间的链接。

2.

幽灵的伤口
并不比纸张割破拇指
留下猩红的曲线
更不显眼
你像鬼魂一样
在众多的奉献中
重演过去

不要告诉我
时间没有维度
理性的智慧
是不能消暑的凉帕
哪怕在废弃的屋子里
空洞的寂静中
也激不起些微的回声。

3.

义务不是爱…的确
怨恨紧随，像海草胶着在

Three of Remembrance

I.

Bitter bone, where sweet the marrow should be,
shallow root, where deep a strange seed wakened.
Landscape in its mystery
aligned with promise
the heart's tethering to pain.
Both recognize their linkage
to the earth's first rain.

II.

A wound of apparition is no less visible
than the scarlet curvature
where paper slits the thumb.
Ghostly, you recapitulate
the past among devotions.

Do not tell me
time has no dimension.
Rational wisdom is the least
cool cloth to the smothering
heat of summer
or the least echo of a voice
at the hallowed silence
of an abandoned room.

III.

Obligation is not love...and yes
resentment clings as seaweed
to the surf-sewn rocks.
At seaside in a morning of deception

海水冲刷的岩石上。
在沙滩上，在一个充满欺骗的黎明，
你轻易的交出所属
减轻了因失去产生的重压
那对你的背叛者
许下千年不变的爱的负疚。

you give, in ease, the belonging
that somehow clarified lifts
the weight of loss, guilt
at having sworn to your betrayer
the vow of eternal love.

承诺

Promises

它们仅仅是承诺
那永远束缚在星宿上的誓约
他们是声音，像海星
撬开紧闭的物体
引发心脏内的聚爆，
在界定时间的画面上
涂着抹不去的线条
将喜庆变为痛苦
将肉体化成淤泥

They were only meant to be
promises, those vows of permanent
bondage to stars
they were
voices that could pry like starfish
imploding the heart, stain
with indelible line
the painting that would border time,
turn festivity to pain
and flesh to slime.

那是美的承诺
如此充满了升华
呼吸停滞了
头颅麻木成一堆颜色
血肉之躯窥探到
永生之结局

That was beauty's promise
so filled with exaltation
all breathing stopped
and numbed the skull to color,
flesh given glimpse
of what it might be like
to live forever.

愿望的单子不断加长
不断变窄
该神圣的都神圣了

需要多得

The wish list lengthens, tapering

漫过杯子的边缘
我们分享的每一种滋味
并未少去
而是更加充盈
当每一个活着的生物
从某种半寐的空间醒来
为我们当选为甜美的
石楠花深深感动着

那些面孔，因孤独而神圣
被无穷的痊愈力所打磨
适时地送到这块地方
由一个名字引路
穿过铭刻的材料和模糊的直觉
反映出那洋溢的记忆
最遥远的边缘

漫过杯边的倒影
不需要荫蔽
或腌制的虚妄来保存
那被海水弄得纷沓杂乱脚步
造成的恐慌

承诺是春天的时光
通过我们伸出的手臂
以无比巨大的威慑力
唤醒惊悸
嘴巴嗫唔着银色的唾液
心脏因绝望而窒息

在渐渐逝去的中心
我们认为的存在
其实并不存在

as all that is hallowed,
as all we want
sufficient to the cup's brim
that every taste we share
does not diminish but further fills
as every living presence wakens
some half-sleeping dimension
touched before we were a choice
among the sweetest heathers.

Those faces, sacred now in solitude
honed from an infinite healing
down to this place in time,
guide in a given name
through print and dim perception
reflecting the farthest reach
of our own brimming.

The cup of reflection needs no shadow
or salted illusions to preserve
a panic of scrambled footprints by the sea.

These promises were springtime
wakening seizures through our arms,
so overwhelming
the mouth murmurs with makeshift silver spasm
through the heat's pause of despair

In the weakening center of
all we know exists and is not there.

父亲

父亲,你走了
除了形象的轮廓
在你女儿的脑子里打印成模
像痛苦的涂片
抹上一张不再期待的面孔

你如何将记忆
从它的钳制中剥离?

现实在哪儿沉睡?
渴望温情
去清除皮肤下
顽固喘息着的污迹
随心脏的安排
呼出
它所渴望的
它所隐藏的
为了永久保存那
无可视见的东西

The Father

Father, you are gone

except for outlines of images

patterned in your daughter's brain

like a smear of pain across

an unexpecting face.

How do you shell a memory

from its grasp to remain?

Where do realities sleep

that covet tenderness

to erase the persistent stain

breathing beneath the skin

exhaling as the heart

rearranges what it will covet

what it will hide

to forever preserve what cannot be

made visible.

永恒的序幕

沿着醒来的梦编织的世界
牛蒡子从荚壳里蹦出
诚实的声音在荚缝处留下痕迹
寂静落下俨然如血的盟誓
名字的圣洁涂白了一段对话

Eternal Prologue

Around the woven world of walking dreams
as milkweed driven from its skin
those upright voices staining at the seams
drop silence as a blood vow
white in wordprints of a dialogue

第一个名字是倒下的父亲
旁边是失去选择的母亲
唯有眼神标示出她的意图

生命历程的语言
和饥荒胁迫下的选择
水蛭般吸啜来自异地的种子
在那旋律曲折，目光失明的年代里

你瞧我，成形于藐视法规
漫无边际地孕育出的野草
在我体内停留一阵吧
听听那首古老的摇篮曲

with purity of names

first name fallen father
near a choiceless mother
sight aligned to signal her intent.

The speech of a life span
and famine-driven choices
leeched their seed from other lands
in other tonal twisted blinded times.

You see me, shaped from overgrown
conceptions of weeds that challenge law.
Abide within my body for awhile
and listen to an ancient lullaby

不被宽恕的时光

That Time Not be Forgiven

那不被宽恕的时光
穿过晨光的帷幔
不见太阳，没有芳香油
来沐浴掉皮肤上的铅尘
紧紧依附着每一条缝隙
当手指触摸火焰而阵阵抽痛

没有为天真无邪洒下一滴泪
被屠杀的嘴唇来不及发出一声

时钟放弃了
有规律地指向
那个绝对的时刻

That time not be forgiven
through scrim of morning light,
no visible sun no circle of molten balm
bathes away the sanded skin
clinging in crevices, throbbing
as a finger touched to fire.

Not a tear for innocents
not a voice within their slaughtered mouths.

The clock has abandoned its orderly
pointing to an absolute hour.
Hands leap among prophetic chimes,

指针跳荡在具有预言性的钟声里
划出均衡的距离

金色的手腕像个沦陷的病人
卷起被篡改一通的时间表
直至虚无

那不被宽恕的时光
孕育着种子的子宫在痉挛
只为从我们眼里吐出
相距甚远的模块
它们紧缩、发散的形象
受到自身生理的召唤所挤压
在我们对天堂热望的四周
环绕的光环渐渐衰弱
相抵触的两瓣头颅震颤着
他们象征的表面迸出火花
闪光、燃烧、消逝
然而没有丝毫声响。

shuffle their lengths for equality.

A golden wrist is trapped like a patient
folding garbled timesheets toward not being.
That time not be forgiven
as wombs convulsed with seed
only to disgorge the distancing
templates in our eyes,
as they too tighten and exude
Images constricted by chemical calling
of gift-given selves, the fading
ringing our passion for the heavens,
trembling the clashing halves of skulls
whose symbols sparkling surfaces
glow and flash and fade yet make no sound.

海变

迁徙和思乡
随着脚步声到拉普兰
双眼皮的海岛被冰山冲破
沐浴在洋流里
冲刷我们
和沙蟹在寂静的沙滩上

良久,沙蟹从沙子下钻出
和船帆与蜗牛一起观看
透过驻留在我们眼睛和牙齿里

Sea Change

Migrations and nostalgias
follow the footfall over Lapland
and epicanthic islands broken with bergs
bathing in seaflow that will wash us
with sandcrabs on quiet beaches

later burrowing to watch
with shipsails and snails
the same scrim of exchange
that resident in eye and tooth

共同的雾幔
如此,船上悬挂的钟
报出的时间有了滋味
等待那些将我们从
睡梦中拽出的深深的扭曲

lends time its taste
to all our clocks
poised at embarkations
waiting for those deep contortions
dragging us from sleep.

觉醒

The Wakening

寻找一根细细的柔软的缰绳
将世界拴在海湾
睡梦纤细的手
扭绞成爪子
撕扯笼罩黑暗的帷幕
被肢解了的手背和眼睛
困惑进记忆不全的折磨里

Searching for a thin gentle leash
to keep the world at bay,
delicate hands of dream
gnarl into claws and tear
the cloth that covers dark
and those dismembered arms and eyes
puzzled into half-remembered torments

长驱直入五脏和活着的粘液
高高举起,预言着
明天会带来的伤害
和有限的怜悯的精髓

pushing into organs and living slime
to hold aloft and divine
the woundings of tomorrow
and marrow of allotted mercy

麻木在文字的阴影里
和那能留见夏天一池的清凉
为冬天税收备下羊毛的神秘

numbed into shadows of words
and mystery that keeps in sight
a pool of summer coolness
or wool gather for winter's tithe

一切围绕祈祷的烈焰旋转
一切沉寂在光耀里
我们被涂抹成千篇一律
为了生存
为了暂时分享
稍许制造光亮的
噼啪作响的火炭。

all circle to this fire of prayer
all silent in the sparking
that paints our sameness to survive
and share for a moment
the power to consume
driven small crackling coals
creating light.

晚餐

你追逐着你的晚饭
我奔跑着为了逃命
兔子从伤口里如是说话
哲学家如是听着
琢磨不出它的意思

手臂失去了声音
指头损耗到只剩
曾会说话的手掌
来预测命运

薄薄的眼袋守护着眼睛
我宣誓启程
到达境地,那儿视觉
会告知从未有过的奇迹

彩虹的尽头堆满财宝
淹没只有老人看得见的野性。

体内的心跳
安抚着
能够破译我们存在
的秘密的链扣。

在你的嘴唇
饥荒徘徊着
带有面包的滋味。

Evening Meal

You are running for your supper
I am running for my life
so spoke the rabbit from his wounds
so listened the philosopher
wondering what he said.

Arms have lost articulation,
fingers worn into once-voicing palms
that yielded fortune.

Thin skinned pouches guard the eyes
and I am sworn a journey
to reach where vision
truly tells its miracles
that have not been.

Treasure spilled at rainbow's end
drowns the savagery
only old men see.

Heartbeat from your body
soothes the deciphering
of why we are here.

Upon your mouth, famine
lingers with the taste of bread.

沉重的盖子

谁说话
来维持
漂泊在污水池里
破成两半的
心的生命
那儿绿色的浮渣欢迎春天
四周的土壤在歌唱
和着薄荷香草中窜出的
各种生命匆匆的脚步声
薄荷草就沾上了人的气味
记忆中浸出的树浆
依旧温馨。

有一个声音
作为一个字的影子
尚未在头骨里诞生
就期待着
被潮汐筛滤出的贝壳们听到
爆发于朝朝暮暮的潮汐
永不消退。

谁说话
在充满奇迹的地方
没有野狗
那食肉的动物
去回应胆怯的猿吠
这深浅有度的世界
轻轻的吟唱着
迎和那黑夜里的影子。

大海里蒸发的潮水
以义无反顾的耐心
等待着接受你肌肤的冰凉
温和地沐浴在
无法回避的延缓之中。

Weighted Lids

Who spoke then?
to keep alive the halved heart
floating in a desecrated pond
where green scum welcomes spring
and all surrounding soils sing
with coming of footsteps and softness
of forms among savory grasses
scented by human odors
and soothing presence of sap
spilling from memory.

There was a voice
as shadow of a word
that was not born within the skull
that waited to be heard among shells
sifting now from tide
erupting in each twilight
and would not recede.

Who spoke then?
timid barking when no wild dogs–those
predators who would answer–existed
in a place of wonder
where a fathomable world
hums softly to affirm
its evening shadows.

Tides distilled from the sea
wait with irretrievable patience
the cool sanction to your skin
the soft bathing of inevitable reprieve.

于无极处

我的孩子们的孩子们
在寂静的池水上飘悠
浑身闪烁着湿气
那儿百合花颤抖着
那儿蜥蜴和青蛙
跌跌撞撞,逃出捕食者绿色的陷阱
倒塌的草丛里藏匿着
乌龟瞪大眼睛的睡眠。

秘密

冬天倾听着
圆石以它的节奏
消蚀了紧敷着的色彩
所绘如所见。

人们曾像我一样
说着空洞的话
祈求得不到的东西

被降托给地衣的神灵
背叛或肯定了
马蹄和人手的回音留下的笔迹
包含即成的契约
从此地到彼地
从石头到木头大厦
荫蔽,欢迎雨季。

So Far Beyond

Children of my children
float with reflected wetness
on the surface of a stilled pond
where lilies tremble
where lizard and frog
tumble through the green
forage of predators,
leaning grasses that contain
the sleep of turtles
shaped with opened eyes.

A Mystery

Winter listens
and round rock in its rhythms
wears away the clinging
colors painted as perceived.

Men once spoke as I
some piece of hallowed prayer
for what could not be given.

Divinities consigned to groundcover
betrayed or affirmed
calligraphies of echoes
left by hoof and hand,
contained the formed indentures
place to place, stone to wooden
edifice that shields and welcomes rain.

出生在楼房里
升华道德的课程
迷失给学问
心跳朝着同一双手
这双手曾为
焦渴的喉咙
和盼望粮食淌成小溪的饥馑
掬捧出甘泉

面孔是一个个奇迹
声音流露出
他们辨认不了的东西。

Born in buildings
the lesson of uplifting
strays into learning.
Heartbeat towards the same cupped hands
once beheld water for parched palates
and thirsts for brooklets of cut grain.

Faces are miracles,
voices reveal what they cannot recognize.

熟睡的小熊

Little Bear Asleep

我爱着这小精灵般的儿子
这爱从未开花在
数十年前
我年轻的体格刚刚成熟

梦的铁盒子里
不再蠕动对过去的怜悯
如今我凝视他
在杂乱无章
灰绿尘封的屋子里
缓缓揭开缚着他的蚕茧

他依偎在小蝌蚪的世界里
萤火虫领着跳舞的飞蛾
排列成神秘的组合
他揪起我手指上的皱皮
那层层沟壑
像山间长满稻子的梯田
看着他自己的手指

I love this phantom son
as never flowered in the decades
when my young construct was begun.

No sympathies for then
writhe within canisters of dream
as now I stare unfolding his cocoon
from rumpled gray-green dusts
that shroud these rooms.
He huddles in his tadpole world
aligning the mysterious gather
of lighting bugs that guide the dancing moths.
He tugs the furrowed skin of my fingers
like a terraced hillside rich with rice
and looks upon his own
with suspicious trembling that my snapshot face
before he had his mother's name

目光怀疑而颤抖
在继承他母亲的姓氏之前
我的面孔不过是一张快照
属于京剧里皇帝们的幽灵

从老式的炉灶里
烤制出狂欢的名字
腐败散发着阵阵恶臭
而天堂温柔的治愈力
古老慈悲，至善至美
在恶意萌生的世界里
我的手祭献出鲜血
供他燃烧
致颂词给他稚嫩的心
于流淌的群山里驿动
在铭刻于心的星辰中
快慰地沐浴。

belonged to a ghost of kings,
phantom from Peking opera of American born.

Stench from this rotten carnival of names,
begotten of archaic ovens
and healing tenderness of heaven,
in perfections of ancient mercy
from a world so ill-conceived,
my hands gift blood to his burning
and to his gentle heart this praise
to pulse in the spill of mountains
and bathe in the solace of remembered stars.

告别昆明

人类,天堂唯一的灾难
给我们犹犹豫豫的影子
倾注了期待和遗憾

四脚兽到直立的两脚兽
伸出弓形手臂去拥抱无穷
犹如湖边扎根的树长出绿色套索
用宝贵的心跳紧缠着
悲剧性的逃亡
逃到漂逝而去的音乐里
时时萦绕被囚禁的呐喊
为着我们一息尚存以来
从未得到的馈赠。

Kunming Goodbye

Human, as only catastrophes of heaven
shower our hesitant shadows with intent
and with regret.

Four-footed ascension upon two,
bow-risen arms reach around infinity
as a green lariat of trees
rooting the edges of a lake
and cling with precious heartbeat
the tragic escape of form
into the drifting musical presence
haunting momentarily a caged cry
of all our breath was never given.

离别的孩子从这张脸前
背过身去
不肯亲吻它的肌肤
他的眼睛燃烧着
高贵地退避于内心
当世界漂泊进记忆的那一刻
空气带着风和种子,张开双翼,
朝着一群消失的鸟飞行
目标锁住战抖的,提供食物的田野
在另一个地方,另一个空间。

A child of departure turns from the face
whose skin he could not kiss
so burning were his eyes
so nobly internalized
that moment when the world drifts away
into memory
airborne with wind and seed, winged
to a flock of fading birds
intent on trembling feeding
in another place, a separate time.

山里出来的女人

Woman Out of Mountains

你,这样神秘
是半个世纪的樟树
是火焰燃烧后的余烬

Such mystery you are
this half century of cinnamon
and cinder.

适婚的岩石和雄性的土地
始终模糊不清
这种伤害使得我们
去拥抱埋在怀里的半张脸
呼吸一些尘土的气味
新鲜散落的头发象瀑布
在里面纯净,熠熠生辉
舌尖蘸到记忆里
尝到失去和得到金羊毛的滋味

Nubile rock and phallic land
remain obscure
the lesions of why we became
to cradle a half-face and breathe
some scent of ash,
pure in the fresh fall of hair
the glow there
tongue-tipped in memory
a taste to determine
dimensions of loss and fleece
or simply one moment
when being uncovers its source
in a woman's flesh

仅仅一瞬间
在一个女人的血肉里
揭示了存在的资源

争取多有一天
不再独立不羁。

to make not-being independent
of another day.

艺术家履历

塞·格瑞瑟,1926 年 5 月生于美国马里兰州巴尔的摩市。

教育:

1949,马里兰大学,动物学学士。

1949–52,毕业于当代艺术学院,雕塑专业,师从 Bill Taylor.

1972,马里兰大学,英美文学硕士。

主要展览:

2006 纽约,布鲁克林,"气" 当代艺术画廊。

1999 马里兰州,索斯伯瑞市,这边独好画廊 (与雕塑家 Michael Winger 同展)。

1995 马里兰州,巴尔的摩市,戈美兹画廊。

1992 华盛顿 D.C.,博耐伯瑞斯克鲁茨涅克国家犹太博物馆,四代雕塑家、雕塑教育家 Alex Giampietro, Bill Taylor, Sy Gresser, Michael Winger 的回顾展。

1986 北卡州,德姆市,杜克大学,布兰特艺术中心(与画家 Charlotte Lichtblau 同展)。

1985 弗吉尼亚州,斯维特布瑞尔市,斯维特布瑞尔画廊。

1977–95 美国驻各国领事馆的陈列:塞内加尔、印度、法国、马达加斯加、墨西哥、英格兰等。

1975 纽约州,纽约市,林肯中心的福德翰大学。

1975 康纳狄克州,纽哈文市,耶鲁大学,伯克利神学中心。

1974 纽约州,纽约市,圣约翰大教堂画廊。

1971 马里兰,巴尔的摩,圣母学院,福瑞尔画廊。

1967 康纳狄克州,纽哈文市,耶鲁大学皮尔森学院。

1961 墨西哥,墨西哥市,圣安吉尔国际展览会。

收藏作品的机构:

纽约市,圣约翰大教堂画廊;

康纳狄克州,耶鲁大学皮尔森学院;

康纳狄克州,费尔菲尔德学院;

康纳狄克州新伦敦,美国艺术博物馆;

弗吉尼亚州阿灵顿,伯斯埃尔犹太教堂;

华盛顿 D.C.,博耐伯瑞斯科鲁茨涅克国家犹太博物馆。

主要发表作品:

《石头、木头、文字——塞·格瑞瑟的艺术作品集》 中国文联出版社,2006。

《海格尔和她的长辈们》 Silver Spring, Maryland, 1990.

《碎片及其他》 LaurelMaryland, 1982.

《儿子们的离别》 Daedal Press, Fallston, Maryland, 1973.

《献给斯蒂文的花环》 Olivant Press, Homestead, Florida, 1971.

《航行记》 Quixote Press, University of Wisconsin, 1969.

《来自墨西哥的诗》 Goosetree Press, Lanham, Maryland, 1964.

《原子武器的到来》 Hennypenny Press, Los Angeles, California, 1957.

《石头的挽歌》 H·H· Walters Publishers, Wales, 1955.

获得的研究基金奖:

华盛顿 D·C.,韦斯里神学院夏季住校雕塑家基金奖;

康纳狄克州,纽哈文市,耶鲁大学夏季住校雕塑家基金奖;

南达科达州,吉斯通,拉希莫山夏季驻留雕塑家基金奖;

纽约州,汉密尔顿,科尔盖特大学夏季驻留研究基金奖;

墨西哥,奥哈卡,美洲组织研究基金奖。

Artist's Resume

Sy Gresser: Born in Baltimore, Maryland, USA, May 9, 1926.

Education:

MS, English & American Literature, Maryland University, 1972.

BS, Zoological Sciences, Maryland University, 1949.

Sculpture, Institute Of Contemporary Arts, Bill Taylor, 1949–52.

Major Exhibitions:

Ch'i Gallery of Contemporary Art, Brooklyn, New York, 2006.

Finer Side Gallery (with sculptor Michael Winger), Salisbury, Maryland, 1999.

G Born omez Gallery, Baltimore, Maryland, 1995.

B'nai Brith Klutznick National Jewish Museum, Washington, D.C., 1992.

Four Generations: Alex Giampietro, Bill Taylor, Sy Gresser, Michael Winger, Retro-spective of Sculpture Teachers, Washington, D.C.

Duke University, Bryant Art Center (With the painter, Charlotte Lichtblau), Durham, North Carolina, 1986.

Sweet Briar College Museum, Sweet Briar, Virginia, 1985.

Arts in Embassies: Senegal, India, France, Madagascar, Mexico, England,

1977–1995.

Fordham University at Lincoln Center, New York City, New York, 1975.

Berkeley Divinity Center at Yale University, New Haven, Connecticut, 1975.

St. John the Divine Cathedral Gallery, New York City, New York, 1974.

Notre Dame College, Fourier Gallery, Baltimore, Maryland, 1971.

Yale University, Pierson College, New Haven, Connecticut, 1967.

San Angel International Exhibition, Mexico, DF, 1961.

Works in private collections:

St. John the Divine Cathedral Gallery;

Yale University Pierson College, Connecticut;

Fairfield College, Fairfield Connecticut;

Museum of American Art, New London, Connecticut;

Beth El Synagogue, Arlington, Virginia;

B'nai Brith Klutznick National Jewish Museum, Washington, D.C.

Major Publications:

Stone, Wood and Words–Collection of Sy Gresser's Art Works, Zhongguo Wen Lian Chu Ban She, China, 2006.

Hagar and Her Elders, Silver Spring, Maryland, 1990.

Fragments & Others, Laurel, Maryland, 1982.

A Departure for Sons, Daedal Press, Fallston, Maryland, 1973.

A Garland for Stephen, Olivant Press, Homestead, Florida, 1971.

Voyages, Quixote Press, University of Wisconsin, 1969.

Poems from Mexico, Goosetree Press, Lanham, Maryland, 1964.

Coming of the Atom, Hennypenny Press, Los Angeles, California, 1957.

Stone Elegies, H. H. Walters Publishers, Wales, 1955.

Residencies/Fellowships:

Wesley Theological Seminary, Summer Sculptor Residence, Washington, D.C.

Yale University, Summer Sculptor in Residence, New Haven, Connecticut;

Mt. Rushmore Summer Sculptor in Residence, Keystone, South Dakota;

Colgate University, Summer Residence, Hamilton, New York;

Organization of American States, Fellowship, Oaxaca, Mexico.